West Chicago Public Library District
118 West Washington
West Chicago, IL 60185-2803
Phone # (630) 231-1552
Fax # (630) 231-1709

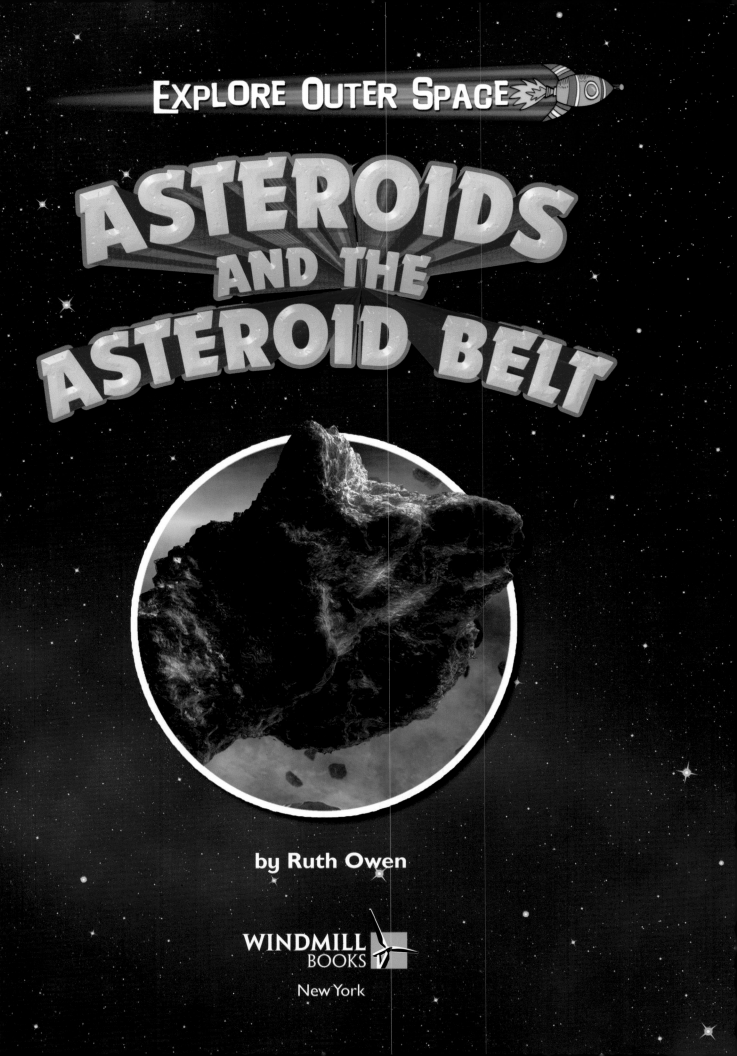

EXPLORE OUTER SPACE

ASTEROIDS
AND THE
ASTEROID BELT

by Ruth Owen

WINDMILL
BOOKS

New York

Published in 2013 by Windmill Books, An Imprint of Rosen Publishing
29 East 21st Street, New York, NY 10010

Produced for Windmill by Ruby Tuesday Books Ltd
Editor for Ruby Tuesday Books Ltd: Mark J. Sachner
US Editor: Sara Antill
Designer: Emma Randall
Consultant: Kevin Yates, Fellow of the Royal Astronomical Society

Photo Credits:
Cover, 1, 4–5, 7 (right), 12–13, 19, 21, 24–25, 28–29 © Shutterstock; 6, 7 (left), 13 (right), 15, 17
18, 20, 26–27 © NASA; 8–9, 14–15, 23 © Science Photo Library; 10–11 © Superstock; 16 ©
NASA/Amanda Diller.

Library of Congress Cataloging-in-Publication Data

Owen, Ruth, 1967–
 Asteroids and the asteroid belt / by Ruth Owen.
    p. cm. — (Explore outer space)
 Includes index.
 ISBN 978-1-4488-8073-7 (library binding) — ISBN 978-1-4488-8115-4 (pbk.) —
ISBN 978-1-4488-8120-8 (6-pack)
 1. Asteroids—Juvenile literature. 2. Asteroid belt—Juvenile literature. I. Title.
 QB651.O94 2013
 523.44—dc23

                                    2011053074

Manufactured in the United States of America

CPSIA Compliance Information: Batch # B3S12WM: For Further Information contact Windmill Books, New York, New York at 1-866-478-0556

CONTENTS

A DATE WITH DISASTER?

A group of scientists and military officers are arguing in the White House. An **asteroid** the size of Texas is just days from colliding with Earth, and no one knows what to do.

Suddenly, a scruffy geek bursts into the room. He has made some mathematical calculations and has a plan that will save the world from disaster!

This may be an exciting plot for a movie, but could Earth one day collide with a giant asteroid?

Astronomers estimate that millions of asteroids may be **orbiting** our Sun. So how did they get there, what do we know about them, and could one of them be heading our way any time soon?

Earth

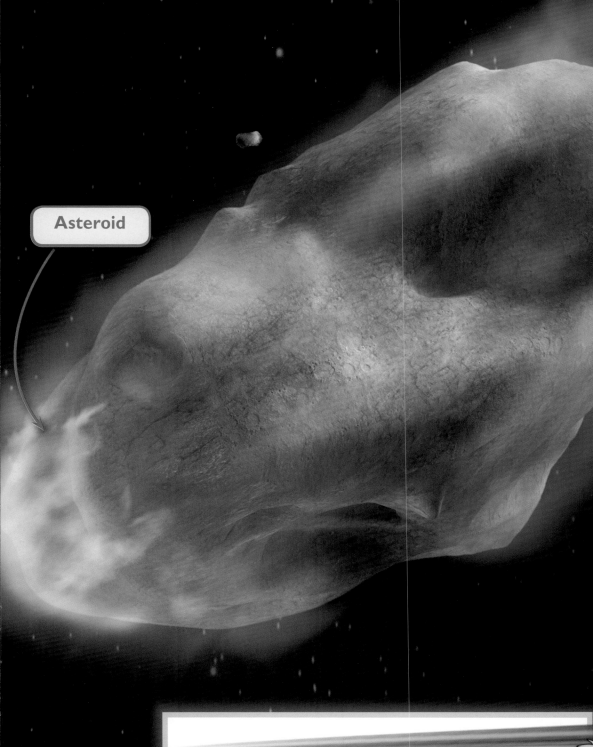

Asteroid

That's Out of This World!

In June 1908, an object with a diameter of around 200 feet (60 m) entered Earth's **atmosphere** and exploded over a part of Russia called Siberia. It destroyed an area of forest larger than half a million football fields!

SPACE ROCKS

Asteroids are Earth's rocky space neighbors. Most are shaped like lumpy potatoes!

Asteroids are made of rocky materials, just like Mercury, Venus, Earth, and Mars. Some also contain metals, such as iron, nickel, and even gold!

Asteroids can be as small as a car, or as large as a mountain. The largest known asteroid, Ceres, has a diameter of 600 miles (966 km)!

The asteroid Eros

This image shows the size of the largest known asteroid, Ceres, in comparison to the Moon.

The Moon

Ceres

That's Out of This World!

Asteroids are not the only bodies that orbit the Sun in our solar system.

Comet	A mixture of ice, rock, and dust that can be as large as 25 miles (40 km) across. Comets often have two bright "tails."
Meteoroid	A chunk of rock—smaller than 3 feet (1 m)—that has broken away from an asteroid or comet.
Meteor	A meteoroid that enters the Earth's atmosphere and burns up. Also called a shooting star.
Meteorite	A meteoroid that lands on the Earth's surface.

MAKING ASTEROIDS

The millions of asteroids orbiting our Sun were created when our solar system formed about 4.5 billion years ago.

Before the solar system came into being, there was a huge cloud of gas and dust in space. Over time, the cloud collapsed on itself. Most of the gas and dust collected around the center of the cloud, creating a massive ball, or sphere. As the sphere rotated, or turned, in space, a disk formed, around the sphere, from the remaining gas and dust.

As all this matter rotated, the sphere pulled in more gas and dust, adding to its size, weight, and **gravity**. The pressure of all the material pressing onto the center of the sphere caused the center to get hotter and hotter. Finally, the temperature inside the sphere got so hot that the sphere ignited to become a star—our Sun!

Inside the rotating disk, other masses formed to become the solar system's planets and their moons. Millions of smaller masses did not fuse together to create planets. Rocky chunks close to the Sun became asteroids, while icy chunks away from the Sun became **comets**.

That's Out of This World!

The word "asteroid" means "like a star" in ancient Greek. Asteroids were given this name because they look like small stars, or points of light, when viewed through a telescope.

Gas and dust

The Sun forming

A planet forming

Asteroids

THE ASTEROID BELT

Asteroids orbit the Sun in many parts of the solar system. Most of them are in a huge area known as the asteroid belt.

The asteroid belt is between the orbits of Mars and Jupiter. In this area, millions of asteroids form a vast, donut-shaped ring.

Sometimes asteroids leave the belt. This may happen when an asteroid is nudged out of its orbit by the powerful gravity of Jupiter, the largest planet in the solar system. Such an asteroid might even end up in an orbit closer to Earth.

Sometimes, when asteroids hit each other, they may break up into pieces. The orbits of these pieces, called **meteoroids**, might cross Earth's orbit. They may even enter Earth's atmosphere as fiery **meteors**, which we call shooting stars!

Larger meteoroids that do not burn up in the atmosphere may land on Earth as **meteorites**.

Asteroids

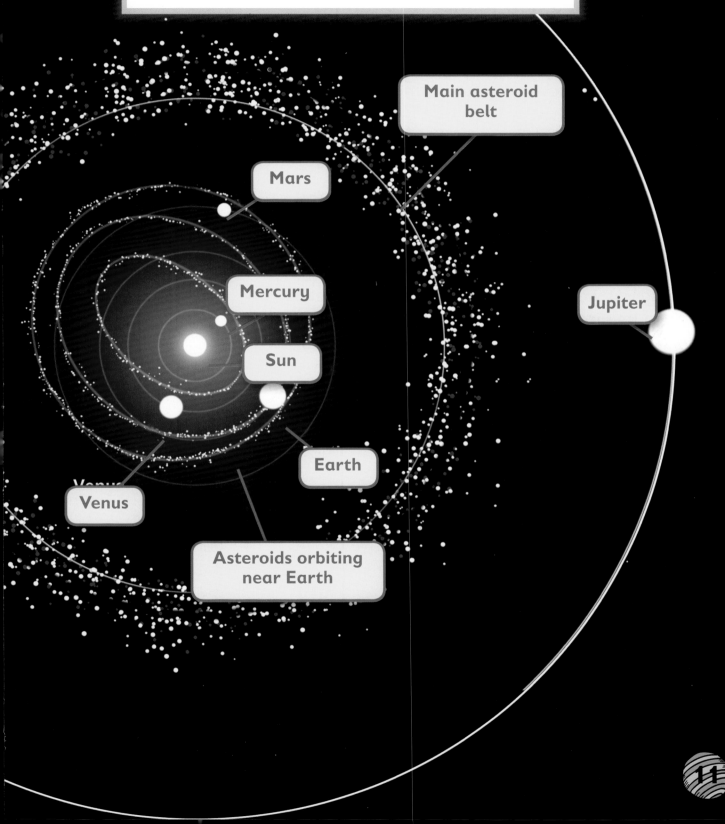

That's Out of This World!

The asteroids on the inner edge of the asteroid belt take about three years to orbit the Sun. Asteroids on the outer edge take up to six years to make one orbit.

Main asteroid belt

Mars

Mercury

Jupiter

Sun

Earth

Venus

Venus

Asteroids orbiting near Earth

THE FIRST KNOWN ASTEROID

On January 1, 1801, an Italian astronomer named **Giuseppe Piazzi** discovered an object orbiting the Sun. Piazzi thought he had seen a new planet through his telescope. In fact, he had found **Ceres**, the first asteroid to be discovered!

Astronomers soon discovered more of these rocky bodies that acted like planets, but were much smaller. Today, over 500,000 asteroids have been found and studied.

In 2006, a group of astronomers called the International Astronomical Union created a new category for space objects that look and act like planets, but are much smaller. Objects in this new category would be known as **dwarf planets**. Since its discovery in 1930, Pluto had been defined as a planet. In 2006, it was redefined as a dwarf planet. In that same year, Ceres, the biggest of all the asteroids, was also defined as a dwarf planet.

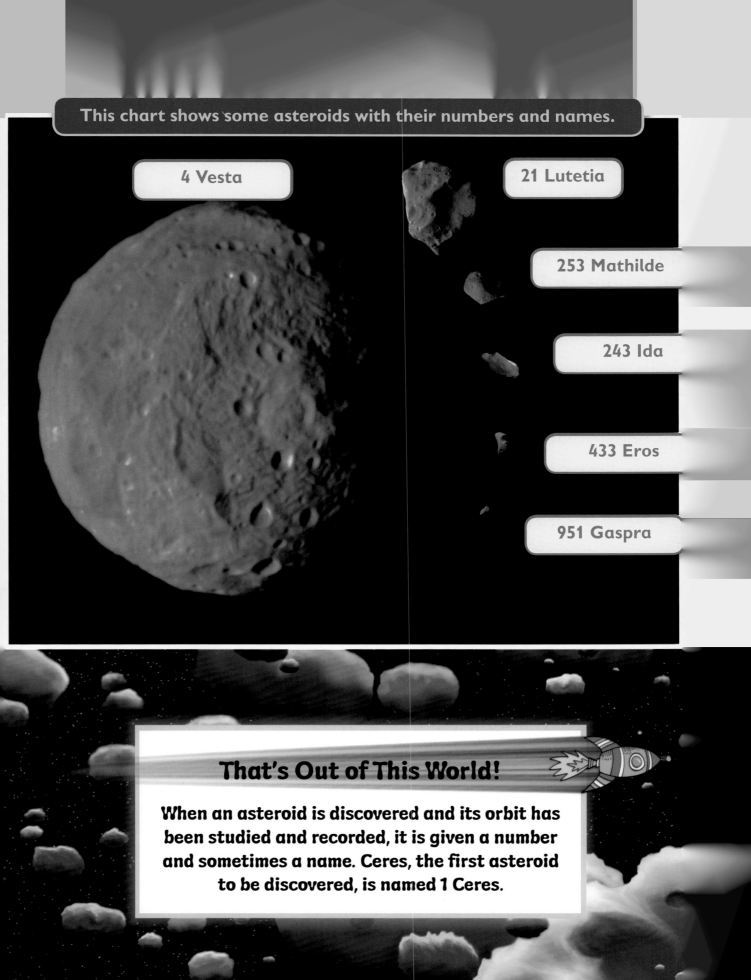

This chart shows some asteroids with their numbers and names.

4 Vesta

21 Lutetia

253 Mathilde

243 Ida

433 Eros

951 Gaspra

That's Out of This World!

When an asteroid is discovered and its orbit has been studied and recorded, it is given a number and sometimes a name. Ceres, the first asteroid to be discovered, is named 1 Ceres.

GETTiNG UP CLOSE WiTH ASTEROiDS

Until the 1990s, astronomers were only able to study asteroids from Earth using telescopes. In 1991, however, the NASA spacecraft *Galileo* took the first-ever close-up photographs of an asteroid!

On its way to Jupiter, *Galileo* photographed the asteroids Gaspra and Ida. *Galileo* also discovered that Ida had its own moon, which was named Dactyl.

In 1996, NASA launched the first-ever space mission designed especially to visit an asteroid. The *NEAR (Near Earth Asteroid Rendezvous) Shoemaker* spacecraft made a flyby of asteroid Mathilde. Then, in 2000, it went into orbit around Eros. *NEAR Shoemaker* transmitted data about Eros and close-up images back to Earth.

On February 12, 2001, *NEAR Shoemaker* touched down on the surface of Eros. Later that month, it shut down its transmissions forever. Eros and its manmade hitchhiker might now be flying through space together for billions of years!

This artwork shows *NEAR Shoemaker* orbiting the asteroid Eros.

That's Out of This World!

When astronomers saw photographs of asteroids, they learned that the surfaces of the asteroids have many **craters**—some that are miles (km) wide! This shows that asteroids have been colliding with each other for billions of years.

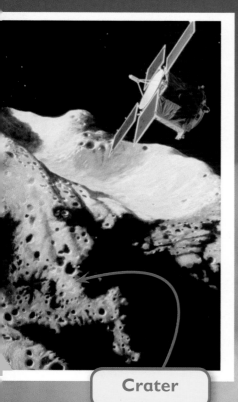

Crater

The rocket carrying *NEAR Shoemaker* blasts off on February 17, 1996

Into the Asteroid Belt

On September 27, 2007, NASA launched the *Dawn* mission. The spacecraft *Dawn* was to travel into the solar system beyond Mars to study and compare Ceres and Vesta, two of the largest bodies in the asteroid belt.

Dawn reached Vesta in July 2011. It was a journey of four years and 1.8 billion miles (2.9 billion km)! Phase two of the *Dawn* mission is to travel another 990 million miles (1.6 billion km) to enter Ceres' orbit in 2015.

Vesta is a dry, rocky body that is similar to Earth and the other planets of the inner solar system. Ceres, however, seems closer in its make-up to icy bodies in the farthest reaches of the solar system. The *Dawn* mission's objective is to learn more about how these two very different asteroids formed, and maybe unlock some of the secrets of how our solar system was formed.

The *Dawn* spacecraft

That's Out of This World!

Dawn will be carrying the names of 365,000 people into the asteroid belt! Space fans were invited to send their names to the *Dawn* project. The names were then etched onto a tiny silicon chip that was attached to the spacecraft.

This illustration shows *Dawn* with Ceres and Vesta. Neither the objects nor their distances from one another are drawn to scale.

Ceres

Vesta

Dawn

Vesta was discovered by German astronomer Heinrich Wilhelm Olbers on March 29, 1807. It was the fourth asteroid to be discovered, so it is officially named "4 Vesta."

The asteroid's surface is made from basaltic rock. This rock was once **lava** that oozed from the hot inside of the asteroid, just as lava pours from a volcano on Earth and then hardens.

On the south pole of Vesta there is a giant crater 285 miles (459 km) across and 8 miles (13 km) deep. At some time in its history, Vesta collided with another space body and a huge chunk of the asteroid broke off, leaving behind the crater. Scientists believe that pieces of Vesta as small as grains of sand and as large as mountains were hurled out into the solar system!

A photograph of Vesta taken by *Dawn* from a distance of 3,231 miles (5,200 km)

That's Out of This World!

Scientists think that some of the **meteorites** that have landed on Earth were once pieces of Vesta. After the asteroid's great collision with another object in space, these rocks were thrown into an orbit that made them collide with Earth.

North America

Vesta

This artwork shows how large Vesta is in comparison to North America.

UP CLOSE WITH CERES

Ceres, which is also considered a dwarf planet, was the first asteroid to be discovered because it was the easiest to see from Earth! If Ceres' diameter of about 600 miles (966 km) is hard to imagine, just think of it as being almost as far across as the width of Texas!

Ceres has a central core of hard material, a mantle, and an outer crust. Scientists believe that the 62-mile-(100 km) thick mantle is made of ice. If this is correct, it would mean that Ceres contains more water than all the freshwater on Earth!

Ceres may also have ice at its north and south poles—just like Earth.

Ceres' layers

Rocky inner core

Thin dusty outer crust

Water-ice mantle

That's Out of This World!

It takes Ceres 4.6 years to make one orbit of the Sun. It rotates on its axis once every 9 hours, 4.5 minutes.

Earth

Ceres

A size comparison between Earth and Ceres

NEAR-EARTH OBJECTS

In 1990, astronomers knew of 182 **Near-Earth Objects (NEOs)**. Today, they have identified and are watching thousands.

An NEO is an asteroid or comet that comes close to the Earth's path around the Sun. For such objects, "close" is within 28 million miles (45 million km). That might seem like a huge distance, but compared with the vastness of space it's not very far at all.

Every day, Earth is hit by a lot of dust and tiny particles from space, but how often does Earth collide with something seriously large?

Scientists estimate that an asteroid or comet about the size of a football field collides with Earth every few hundred years.

Once every few million years, something heads for our planet that has the potential to end all life on Earth!

That's Out of This World!

Astronomers believe there are about 1,000 NEOs with diameters over 0.6 mile (1 km). They classify Near-Earth Objects with diameters over 360 feet (110 m) as potentially hazardous.

This illustration shows what kind of
a shadow a 1-mile-(1.6 km) wide asteroid
might cast as it heads for Earth.

AN EXTINCTION-LEVEL EVENT

In the late 1970s, scientists discovered a huge crater near the town of Chicxulub on the Yucatan Peninsula, in Mexico. The crater was evidence that at some point in our planet's history, something had collided with Earth—something big. Very big!

Over millions of years, the crater had become hidden under layers of rock and soil, but scientists were able to collect data to prove its existence.

Over time, scientists concluded that an asteroid or comet at least 6 miles (9.7 km) wide had collided with Earth about 65 million years ago. The result of this devastating event was the extinction of up to 70 percent of the **species** on Earth—including the dinosaurs!

The collision may have caused huge tidal waves and earthquakes and thrown up vast clouds of incredibly hot ash and steam that covered the skies across the planet.

That's Out of This World!

The crater near Chicxulub is one of the largest on Earth at 3,000 feet (914 m) deep and at least 112 miles (180 km) wide.

COLLISION COURSE

With thousands of known Near-Earth Objects in orbits close to our planet, what's being done to keep track of these rocky neighbors, and how do we know when a new hazard moves into our space neighborhood?

NASA and other space organizations are constantly watching the skies for new objects that have moved from elsewhere in the solar system and are now orbiting close to Earth. When a new NEO is discovered, its orbit is plotted into the future to enable scientists to see if the object will ever be on a collision course with Earth.

So what could be done if a large NEO was heading for Earth? A spacecraft could be flown into the asteroid to knock it off course. A robotic craft, known as a "gravity tractor" could also be sent to cruise alongside the asteroid. The craft's gravity would pull the asteroid off course so that it missed Earth.

That's Out of This World!

In July 2005, NASA deliberately flew a spacecraft into a comet, Tempel 1, in order to find out what materials are inside the comet. The *Deep Impact* spacecraft's lander, which is called an impactor, hit the comet. The *Deep Impact* flyby probe took pictures and collected data from the debris that flew out of the comet.

Deep Impact impactor

Deep Impact
flyby probe.

Comet Tempel 1

27

LOOKING TO THE FUTURE

On November 8, 2011, an asteroid the size of an aircraft carrier made its closest approach to Earth in 200 years.

The asteroid, called 2005 YU55, was just 201,700 miles (324,600 km) from Earth! It was the largest Near-Earth Object to come this close to Earth in about 30 years. YU55 is just one of thousands of Near Earth Objects that scientists continue to track. By studying them and understanding their orbits they can rule out any potential danger to our planet.

At this moment in time, thanks to astronomers and monitoring systems around the world, we can be sure that there is no threat of Earth colliding with any of the known Near-Earth Objects for at least the next 100 years.

For now, our little place in the solar system is safe. The only giant asteroids heading for Earth are the ones in the movies!

That's Out of This World!

While a new, potentially hazardous object might enter Earth's orbit and hit Earth in the future, scientists think the chances of this happening in the next 100 years are very small.

GLOSSARY

asteroid (AS-teh-royd) A rocky object orbiting the Sun and ranging in size from a few feet (m) to hundreds of miles (km) in diameter.

asteroid belt (AS-teh-royd BELT) A region of the solar system between the orbits of Mars and Jupiter where the largest number of known asteroids orbit the Sun.

astronomers (uh-STRAH-nuh-merz) Scientists who specialize in the study of outer space.

atmosphere (AT-muh-sfeer) The layer of gases surrounding a planet, moon, or star.

comet (KAH-mit) An object orbiting the Sun consisting primarily of a nucleus, or center, of ice and dust and, when near the Sun, tails of gas and dust particles pointing away from the Sun.

craters (KRAY-turz) Holes or dents in the surface of a planet, moon, or other space object, usually caused by an impact with another space object.

dwarf planets (DRAWF PLA-nets) Objects in space that have certain characteristics that distinguish them from other bodies orbiting the Sun. One of these is that the object be large enough and its gravity be strong enough to have caused it to become nearly round. Also, its orbit around the Sun cannot have been swept clear of other bodies, as would be the case with the larger planets, and it must not be a moon of a larger planet.

gravity (GRA-vuh-tee) The force that causes objects to be attracted toward Earth's center or toward other physical bodies in space, such as stars or planets.

lava (LAH-vuh) Rock that has been heated within a planet, moon, or asteroid to the point where it flows like a liquid.

meteorites (MEE-tee-uh-rytz) Pieces of asteroids that have survived the fall to the surface of a planet or moon.

meteoroids (MEE-tee-uh-roydz)
small particles or fragments that
have broken free from an asteroid.

meteors (MEE-tee-orz) The streaks
of light made by meteoroids or other
pieces of dust or rock from space
burning up in Earth's atmosphere;
may also refer to the body itself as
it burns up and its path across the
atmosphere becomes visible.

Near-Earth Objects
(NEER-urth OB-jekts) Asteroids or
comets that come within 28 million
miles (45 million km) of the Earth's
orbit around the Sun.

orbiting (OR-bih-ting) Circling in a
curved path around another object.

solar system (SOH-ler SIS-tem)
The Sun and everything that orbits
around it, including asteroids,
meteoroids, comets, and the planets
and their moons.

species (SPEE-sheez) A group
of plants, animals, or other living
organisms that are similar genetically
and may reproduce with other
members of the same group.

WEBSITES

**For web resources related to the subject of this book,
go to: www.windmillbooks.com/weblinks
and select this book's title.**

READ MORE

Aguilar, David. *13 Planets: The Latest View of the Solar System*. Des Moines, IA: National Geographic Kids, 2011.

Kortenkamp, Steve. *Asteroids, Comets, and Meteoroids*. Fact Finders: The Solar System and Beyond. Mankato, MN: Capstone Press, 2011.

Sparrow, Giles. *Destination Asteroids, Comets, and Meteors*. Destination Solar System. New York: PowerKids Press, 2010.

INDEX